Contents

Words in **bold** are in the glossary on page 31.

What is a Rainforest?

Rainforests are areas of thick forest where it rains nearly all year round. They are home to more than half of all the millions of types of plants and animals on Earth.

► *This map shows the areas of tropical and temperate rainforest worldwide. Although they only cover a small part of the Earth, they are home to more than half of all living things.*

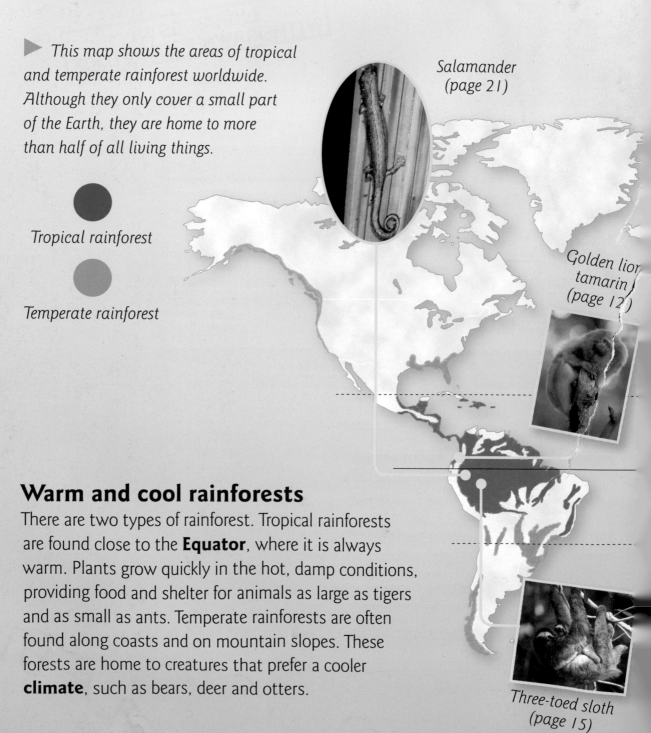

● Tropical rainforest

● Temperate rainforest

Salamander
(page 21)

Golden lion
tamarin
(page 12)

Three-toed sloth
(page 15)

Warm and cool rainforests

There are two types of rainforest. Tropical rainforests are found close to the **Equator**, where it is always warm. Plants grow quickly in the hot, damp conditions, providing food and shelter for animals as large as tigers and as small as ants. Temperate rainforests are often found along coasts and on mountain slopes. These forests are home to creatures that prefer a cooler **climate**, such as bears, deer and otters.

EXTREME ANIMALS

The Goliath bird-eating spider of the South American rainforest is the largest spider in the world. Some of them are bigger than a dinner plate!

30 cm

A high-rise home

Rainforests are divided into layers. At the bottom is the dark, damp forest floor, where creatures such as spiders, scorpions and beetles live. Above this, there are small trees and bushes growing towards the sunlight. The tops of the trees are called the **canopy**. This layer of the rainforest is buzzing with life. Monkeys swing between the trees, butterflies flutter among the flowers and snakes curl around the branches. Above the very tallest trees, eagles soar — looking for prey in the canopy below.

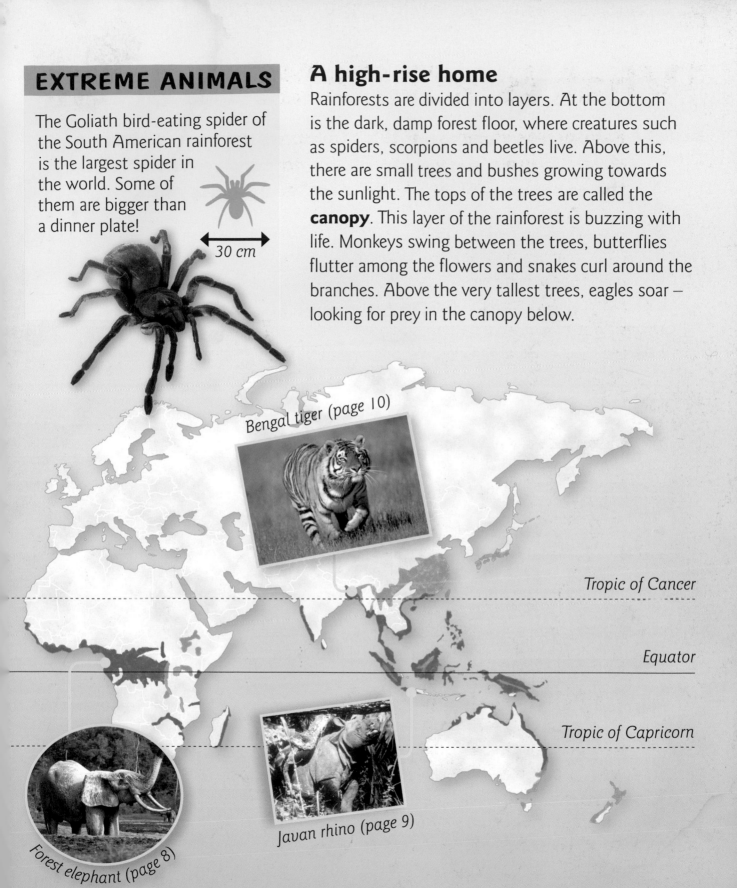

Bengal tiger (page 10)

Tropic of Cancer

Equator

Tropic of Capricorn

Javan rhino (page 9)

Forest elephant (page 8)

Rainforests Under Threat

Huge areas of the world's rainforests are being cut down. People want the land to live on, to grow crops and to graze livestock. They also want to make use of the wood from the trees.

Homeless and hungry

People are worried about the destruction of the rainforests because it contributes to **global warming**, but the destruction also has a huge effect on the forest animals. Without the trees, many creatures lose their homes. The flowers, fruit and leaves of the trees also provide food for millions of animals. No trees means no food.

▼ *Cutting down the rainforests affects the environment as well as leaving animals without food or shelter.*

WHAT DO YOU THINK?

In Southeast Asia, parts of the rainforest are being cut down to make way for oil palm **plantations**. The oil is sold for use in food products across the world. What arguments do you think there are for and against using rainforest land in this way?

Separation and competition

When parts of the rainforest are cleared, groups of animals can become separated from others of their **species**. This is called **fragmentation**, and it reduces the number of potential mates for the animals. As more creatures are forced to live in smaller areas of forest, there is greater competition for food, water and shelter. There may not be enough to go around.

Human hunters

Hunting is also a threat to rainforest animals such as tigers, caimans and rhinos. Some people kill them for their valuable meat, fur or horns, but others just hunt them for sport. The people who live in and around the rainforests are often respectful of their environment, but sometimes they feel they must cut down the trees or kill the animals to survive.

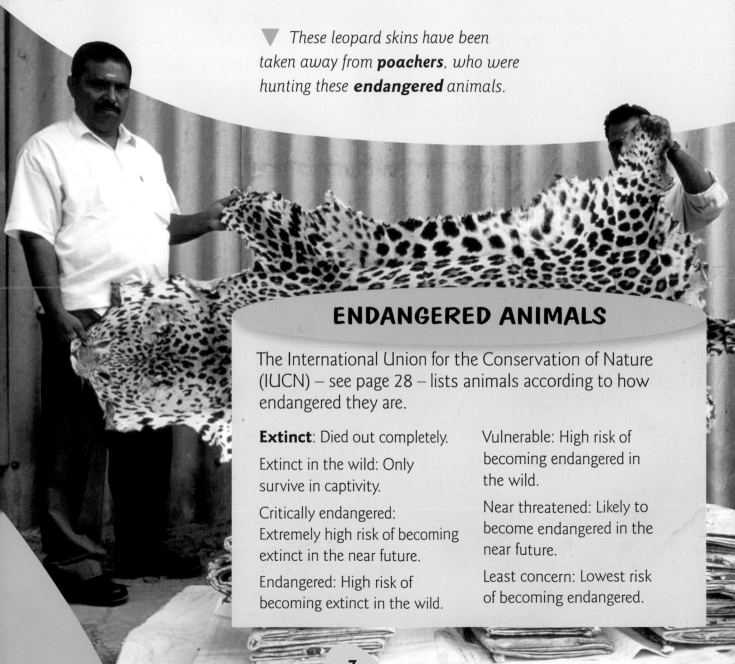

▼ *These leopard skins have been taken away from* **poachers***, who were hunting these* **endangered** *animals.*

ENDANGERED ANIMALS

The International Union for the Conservation of Nature (IUCN) – see page 28 – lists animals according to how endangered they are.

Extinct: Died out completely.

Extinct in the wild: Only survive in captivity.

Critically endangered: Extremely high risk of becoming extinct in the near future.

Endangered: High risk of becoming extinct in the wild.

Vulnerable: High risk of becoming endangered in the wild.

Near threatened: Likely to become endangered in the near future.

Least concern: Lowest risk of becoming endangered.

Nature's Heavyweights

Large mammals find it hard to move between the tightly packed trees in the rainforest so most live in more open areas. However, a few big beasts have adapted to the rainforest habitat.

Endangered elephants

Herds of forest elephants roam through the African rainforests, but their **habitat** has been destroyed or fragmented, and they are hunted for their **ivory** tusks. Organisations such as WWF (see page 28) are campaigning to stop illegal **poaching** and to protect the elephants' rainforest home.

▼ *Forest elephants are smaller than their grassland cousins. They have darker skin for better **camouflage**, and their tusks are straighter to stop them getting caught in the thick undergrowth.*

WHAT DO YOU THINK?

In some parts of the world, rainforests are being cleared to make way for farmland so people can earn money to feed their families. How might these human needs be met without ignoring the needs of rainforest animals?

Little hippos

Hunting and forest clearance means that fewer than 3,000 pygmy hippos survive in the steamy **swamps** of West Africa's rainforests. All is not lost for these little hippos, though. The International Union for Conservation of Nature is hoping to make Liberia's hippo habitat a protected area, and they are being bred in zoos all over the world.

▶ *Adult pygmy hippos weigh up to 275 kg, while common hippos can reach 3,600 kg.*

Rare rhinos

There are five species of rhinoceros and all of them are endangered. The two most threatened types are the Sumatran and Javan rhinos, which live in the rainforests of Indonesia. Groups all over the world are fighting to stop them dying out, including the International Rhino Foundation and WWF. They conduct research, help prevent poaching and conserve the rainforest habitat.

SAVING WILDLIFE

Javan rhinoceros
With only 40–60 animals left in Java and Vietnam, the Javan rhino is one of the world's most endangered animals. Although everything possible is being done to protect them, experts are afraid that it may be too late to save them from extinction.

Big Cats

Cats can move quietly after their prey through the shadowy darkness of the rainforest. They are also good at climbing so they can move around in the treetops, too.

Bengal tiger

In 1900, there were more than 50,000 Bengal tigers but now there are only 2,500 in the rainforests and grasslands of Asia. They were killed by hunters, and many died as the forests were cut down. The Indian government has set up 66 protected areas, where tiger habitats are conserved. Guards patrol here to deter illegal poaching. These measures may save the tiger from extinction.

Cats in crisis

Nearly all the big cats of the rainforest are now endangered. Some of them, such as the clouded leopard of Asia, are hunted for their body parts. Tigers, jaguars and leopards are under threat because their habitat is being destroyed. As they move into smaller areas of rainforest, there may not be enough food to go around.

Cat conservation

Hunting big cats is now banned in most places. To increase their numbers, some cats may be bred in zoos or wildlife **reserves**. This is called **captive breeding**. It does not always work, though. For example, in zoos male clouded leopards often kill the females before they can breed.

▶ *The jaguar's spotted fur provides good camouflage in the rainforest.*

WHAT DO YOU THINK?

Big cats such as tigers, leopards and jaguars are popular attractions in zoos. Some people say it is cruel to keep them in captivity but others argue that it helps **conservation** efforts. What do you think?

Forest Monkeys and Apes

The rainforest is alive with the calls of many different monkeys and apes, from tiny marmosets to big chimps. It's the perfect home for these treetop travellers.

Great apes

All species of ape can be found in the rainforests of Africa or Southeast Asia – gorillas, chimpanzees, bonobos, orangutans and gibbons – and most of them are endangered. Some, such as gibbons, are hunted for their body parts, which are used in Asian medicine. Others struggle to survive in the shrinking areas of available forest.

▶ *All species of gibbon are endangered because of hunting and the destruction of their rainforest home.*

Life in the treetops

Most monkeys live in the canopy, swinging between the trees using their long, strong arms. They can find all the food and shelter they need among the branches, so many of them never come down. Unfortunately this means that some species have been badly affected by forest clearance. Human **predators** are also a threat. Hunted for its beautiful fur, the golden lion tamarin was nearly extinct by the 1970s, but conservation and captive breeding helped the species survive, and there are now more than 1,000 in the wild.

◀ *Golden lion tamarins are recovering from near-extinction.*

SAVING WILDLIFE

Orangutan

Experts think that there are fewer than 50,000 wild orangutans left – a fifth of the number there were 100 years ago – because of hunting, **deforestation** and **wildfires**. These apes can only be found in Sumatra and Borneo, where organisations such as the Orangutan Foundation International are helping save them by planting new trees, preventing illegal mining and educating locals about the importance of the apes.

Tree-Dwellers

The rainforest canopy is so rich with fruit, nuts, leaves and insects that many animals can get all the food they need in the treetops, without ever having to hunt on the forest floor.

Animals of the canopy

Some of the most curious creatures of the rainforest spend their lives in the tree canopy. The rare binturong of Asia uses its long, muscular tail to grip on to branches when **foraging** for food. In Madagascar, the unusual aye-aye draws out bugs from trees by tapping on the trunk like a woodpecker. Aye-ayes are killed by local people, who think they are bad luck.

▲ *Binturongs have been nicknamed bearcats, although they do not belong to either the bear or cat families.*

▲ *Algae grows on a sloth's fur to help it blend in with the tree it lives in.*

Sleepy creatures

Sloths are famous sleepyheads – they hardly move at all. They might come to the ground occasionally, but they are slow-moving and easy prey for big cats and birds of prey such as eagles. To stay out of sight, sloths are **nocturnal**. During the day they stay very still, sleeping upside down on their branches for up to 20 hours a day!

EXTREME ANIMALS

Aye-ayes of the Madagascan rainforest are the only surviving member of the animal family scientists call *Daubentoniidae*.

Lizards Large and Small

Reptiles are cold-blooded, getting the warmth they need to survive from their environment, so tropical rainforests are a favourite place for animals such as lizards and crocodiles.

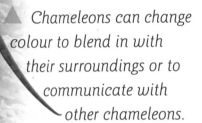

▲ *Chameleons can change colour to blend in with their surroundings or to communicate with other chameleons.*

Little lizards

All sorts of lizards have adapted to life in the rainforest, from giant water monitors to tiny geckos. Iguanas and chameleons have long, sharp claws and long tails that help them grip tree branches. Some can jump from tree to tree in great leaps. Most lizards feed on the plentiful plants and insects, so few are endangered at present.

EXTREME ANIMALS

Flying lizards of Southeast Asia don't actually fly – they use special flaps of skin to help them glide through the rainforest canopy.

Crocs in the swamps

Crocodiles and caimans lurk in rainforest swamps, feeding on turtles and fish. Their skins are highly prized by hunters, so several species are now endangered, including the black caiman of the Amazon and the small African slender-snouted crocodile.

▼ *Scientists release young Orinoco crocodiles back into the wild in Venezuela.*

SAVING WILDLIFE

Orinoco crocodile

The largest predator in South America is also one of the rarest. There are only 250–700 Orinoco crocodiles left, so they are now a protected species. The Wildlife Conservation Society began a captive-breeding programme in the 1990s. Many crocs have been released into the wild, where they are monitored carefully to make sure the males don't kill each other before they can breed.

Tropical Snakes

Snakes are found on every continent except Antarctica – and in a wide range of habitats – but they are most at home in the warm, wet rainforests.

Emerald tree boas use their colouring to hide in trees so their prey doesn't spot them.

Snakes everywhere

Snakes can be found in most layers of the rainforest. Some coil themselves around branches in the canopy, while others hide in the thick undergrowth or make burrows beneath the soil. There are even some snakes that live in rainforest rivers. Tree snakes like the emerald tree boa, found in the rainforests of South America, tend to be green or brown so they blend in with their leafy habitat. Others, such as the coral snake, have bright colours or patterns on their skin. This is a warning that they are poisonous, to stop larger animals eating them.

Finding food

Most snakes feed on the plentiful supply of birds, bats, frogs and insects, but some, such as huge pythons and boa constrictors, can eat much bigger animals. Whatever their favourite snack, when the trees are cut down all these creatures die or move away, and the snakes' food supply dwindles.

◀ *African bush vipers ambush their prey by hanging from the trees and injecting their victim with venom from their fangs.*

SAVING WILDLIFE

Jamaican boa

As forests are destroyed on the Caribbean island of Jamaica, boas have been forced into more inhabited areas. People also kill them because they think the snakes are poisonous. The Durrell Wildlife Conservation Trust operates one of the most successful captive-breeding programmes. Hundreds of captive-bred snakes have now been released into the wild, and it is likely that this species will be saved from becoming more endangered.

EXTREME ANIMALS

The huge anaconda is the largest snake in the Amazon rainforest, growing up to 9 m long.

Amphibians

Brilliantly coloured frogs, salamanders and worm-like caecilians are the three main types of amphibian that live in the rainforest. The air is so full of moisture that they don't need pools of water to survive, as amphibians do in other habitats.

Threatened frogs

There are more types of frog in the rainforest than any other **amphibian**, but they are also the most threatened. The bright colours and poisonous nature of many frogs keeps most predators at bay, but more than 100 species have become extinct in the past 30 years because of **climate change**, habitat loss and disease.

◀ *Frogs are among the most colourful of all rainforest creatures. This is a red-eyed tree frog in Central America.*

EXTREME ANIMALS

The golden poison frog of Colombia contains enough poison to kill several humans.

2.5 cm

SAVING WILDLIFE

Poison dart frog

These tiny amphibians are highly toxic – so much so that South American rainforest tribes would tip their hunting spears with the poison. There are many types of poison dart frog, and several of them are threatened by a fungal disease. Conservation programmes focus on capturing and treating frogs that have the disease, to stop it spreading.

◀ *Poison dart frogs release a poison through their skin.*

Salamanders in a warming world

Most salamanders are found in the world's temperate rainforests, but there has been a big drop in their numbers in the past 30 years. Although habitat loss accounts for some of this, experts think they have been more affected by climate change. There is some good news, though: in 2008, three previously unknown salamander species were discovered in the Costa Rican rainforests – and there may be more still undiscovered.

▶ *Salamanders such as the* Bolitoglossa peruviana *of Ecuador and Peru have webbed feet, so they can cling to smooth surfaces like leaves.*

Minibeasts

Insects are important in the rainforest because they help keep the soil healthy and the flowers pollinated. They also provide food for many larger creatures.

▲ *Wasp colony in the Amazon rainforest.*

▲ *These shield bugs in Madagascar release a smelly liquid to stop them being eaten.*

▼ *Rhino beetle from Malaysia.*

Alive with insects

Huge spiders make their homes on the forest floor and in the trees. Colourful beetles scuttle among the leaves. Ants and termites live in large colonies. Experts think there may be millions of insect species in the rainforest that have not even been discovered! They all contribute to the balance of the rainforest **ecosystem**.

Insects under threat

Some insects eat just one type of plant, so if that plant is lost from the forests they have no food. Creepy-crawlies that make their homes in the ground are affected by soil **erosion**. Protecting the rainforests will keep these creatures safe from extinction.

▶ *This colourful weevil sits on a leaf in the rainforest of Papua New Guinea.*

▲ *Banana spider in Hawaii.*

SAVING WILDLIFE

Queen Alexandra's birdwing

The Queen Alexandra's birdwing is the largest butterfly in the world, but it can now only be found in a small area of rainforest in Papua New Guinea. They have been hunted by collectors and the forest has been cut down for use as farmland. It is now against the law to trade them, and their habitat is protected, so their numbers are rising again.

31 cm

▶ *Jewel beetles, such as this one from Malaysia, are highly prized by insect collectors.*

In the Air

In the branches of the rainforest trees thousands of colourful birds feed and breed. High above, birds of prey circle, waiting to swoop on unsuspecting animals below.

Parrot paradise

Brilliantly coloured parrots and toucans are a familiar sight in tropical rainforests. They eat nuts, berries and insects, and raise their young in tree hollows. While these birds suffer from habitat loss, the biggest danger comes from human hunters, capturing them to be sold as pets.

◀ *Hyacinth macaws, from the Amazon, came under threat because of deforestation and because local tribes killed them to sell their feathers to tourists.*

SAVING WILDLIFE

Hyacinth macaw
While many macaws are already extinct, the hyacinth macaw is making a comeback from its threatened status. Working with Brazilian authorities, WWF has helped the number of wild hyacinth macaws nearly double in the past 30 years. There are now around 6,500.

▶ *Toucans live in the rainforests of Central and South America.*

Bats in the night

At night the rainforest air is thick with bats, from giant flying foxes to tiny bumblebee bats, smaller than a human thumb. Some bat species are especially important to the rainforest ecosystem because they **pollinate** the flowers.

▲ *Flying foxes and other bats use their clawed feet to hang upside down from branches while sleeping.*

Birds of prey

Birds of prey such as hawks, eagles and vultures all live in the rainforest, nesting in the branches of the tallest trees. The harpy eagle of Central and South America is one of the largest – so big that it can catch and carry creatures such as iguanas and sloths.

Harpy eagle

WHAT DO YOU THINK?

Harpy eagles are a threatened species, but they prey on other endangered rainforest animals such as sloths. Is there a natural order in the wild that we shouldn't interfere with?

In the Water

Rainforests are filled with water, from small pools to great rivers. A huge variety of freshwater creatures exist here, from exotic fish to turtles and even dolphins.

◀ Colourful tropical fish live in rainforest rivers and coastal waters

Tropical fish

Bright tropical fish flash through the warm forest waters, sharing their habitat with larger species such as electric eels. Recent reports suggest that some species of tropical fish are dying out because they cannot adapt to the rise in water temperatures caused by global warming.

EXTREME ANIMALS

The piranha is the world's deadliest fish. A school of piranhas can strip a victim to the bone in minutes.

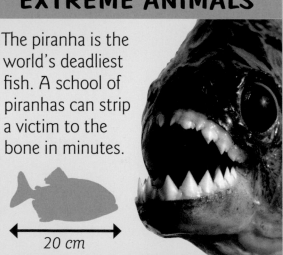

20 cm

Pink river dolphins

Pink river dolphins are one of the creatures affected by the loss of fish in the rainforest waters because they are its main source of food. These Amazonian dolphins are not yet endangered, but they might be in the future if people don't act now to solve the problems of water pollution and dwindling fish stocks.

▶ *Little is known about pink river dolphins, so a lot of research is needed to help in their conservation.*

SAVING WILDLIFE

Manatee

The manatee is the largest marine **mammal** in the Amazon. Manatees are considered vulnerable to extinction because of pollution, hunting and dam-building. Conservation programmes have included rescuing ill or injured manatees and reducing water pollution. But the best hope for the manatee's future is the overall protection of the South American rainforests.

◀ *Manatees look a bit like seals, but their closest living relative is the elephant!*

What Can We Do?

People are more aware than ever before of the threats to rainforest animals, and all over the world there are campaigns to protect this precious environment. Sometimes national governments take steps to protect their endangered creatures. International organisations work with local communities to make a difference. But even individuals can help save rainforest wildlife.

Find out more...

WWF (*www.wwf.org.uk*)
Here you can follow links to information on all sorts of endangered animals and find out what WWF is doing in the world's tropical regions to save these creatures.

Wildlife Conservation Society (*www.wcs.org*)
This American organisation manages conservation projects, research and education programmes all over the world. Their website will tell you all about the animals it is working to save, including forest elephants, tigers and jaguars.

EDGE of Existence (*www.edgeofexistence.org*)
The EDGE of Existence is a special global conservation programme that focuses on saving what it calls 'evolutionary distinct and globally endangered' (EDGE) species. These are unusual animals and plants that are under threat.

International Union for Conservation of Nature (*www.iucn.org*)
The IUCN produces the Red List, which lists all the world's known endangered species and classifies them by how threatened they are, from least concern to extinct. You can see the whole list of endangered animals on the website.

Convention on International Trade in Endangered Species (*www.cites.org*)
CITES is an international agreement between governments that makes sure trade in wild animal species does not threaten their survival. It lists animals that are considered to be under threat from international trading, and makes laws accordingly.

Rainforest Alliance
(*www.rainforest-alliance.org*)
Find out about the work of Rainforest Alliance, an international non-profit organisation working to conserve biodiversity and ensure sustainable livelihoods.

Do more...

Sign a petition

Petitions are documents asking governments or organisations to take action on something people are concerned about. Some of the organisations opposite have online petitions that you can sign to show your support for their campaigns.

Go to the zoo

Find out if your local zoo is involved in any captive-breeding programmes and go along to find out more. Just visiting the zoo helps support these important programmes.

Adopt an animal

For a small contribution to some conservation organisations you get to 'adopt' a rainforest animal. They will send you information about your adopted animal and keep you up to date on all the conservation efforts in the area.

Spread the word

Find out as much as you can about the threats to rainforest animals and what people are doing to save them, then tell your friends and family. The more support conservation organisations have, the more they can do!

Read more...

Rainforests
(Research on the Edge)
by Louise Spilsbury
(Wayland, 2014)

Very Wonderful, Very Rare –
Saving the Most Endangered
Wildlife on Earth
by Baillie and Butcher
(Franklin Watts, 2013)

30 Million Different Insects
in the Rainforest
(The Big Countdown)
by Paul Rockett
(Franklin Watts, 2014)

Eco Alert: Rainforests
by Rebecca Hunter
(Franklin Watts, 2010)

Rainforest Animals Quiz

See how much you can remember about rainforest animals by taking the quiz below. Look back through the book if you need to. The answers are on page 32.

1. What are the two main types of rainforest?

2. What is the name given to the upper layer of the rainforest?

3. Why are people cutting down the rainforests?

4. What is the most endangered type of rhino?

5. Why are clouded leopards being hunted?

6. Which ape is hunted for its body parts?

7. What is the slowest-moving mammal in the world?

8. What is the proper name for the bearcat?

9. Which rainforest lizard can change colour?

10. What do rainforest crocodiles feed on?

11. What do bright colours on a snake usually mean?

12. What are the greatest threats to rainforest frogs?

13. In which country were new species of salamander recently discovered?

14. What is the largest butterfly in the world?

15. Why are insects important to the rainforest ecosystem?

16. What is the biggest threat to parrots in the rainforest?

17. Which bat is the size of a thumb?

18. What environmental issue is   most affecting tropical fish?

19. Why might pink river dolphins
    soon be under threat?

20. What is the manatee's closest
    living relative?

Glossary

adapted changed in order to survive in new conditions.

amphibian a cold-blooded animal that spends some of its life on land and some in water.

camouflage the colour or patterns on an animal that help it blend in with its surroundings.

canopy the layer of the rainforest made up of the branches and leaves in the tops of the trees.

captive breeding when endangered animals are specially bred in zoos or wildlife reserves so that they can then be released back into the wild.

climate the regular pattern of temperature and weather conditions in a particular area.

climate change a difference in the expected weather conditions or temperatures across the world.

cold-blooded cold-blooded animals cannot regulate their own body temperature like mammals do, but instead get their warmth from their environment.

conservation efforts to preserve or manage habitats when they are under threat, have been damaged or destroyed.

deforestation the cutting down of large areas of forest.

domestic tamed by humans; domestic animals are often kept as pets or livestock.

ecosystem all the different types of plants and animals that live in a particular area together with the non-living parts of the environment.

endangered at risk of becoming extinct.

Equator an imaginary line around the middle of the Earth that separates the world into the Northern and Southern hemispheres.

erosion the wearing away of rock or soil, for example by the motion of water or wind, over a period of time.

extinct when an entire species of animal dies out, so that there are none left on Earth.

foraging searching for food or other provisions such as material to build nests or burrows.

fragmentation the breaking up of areas of rainforest by cutting down the trees between them.

global warming the rise in average temperatures around the world as a result of human activity such as deforestation.

habitat the place where a plant or animal lives.

ivory the hard, smooth substance that elephant tusks are made from.

livestock animals kept by people for meat or milk.

logging cutting down trees in the rainforest to sell the wood for building or other uses.

mammals warm-blooded animals that give birth to live young.

nocturnal active at night.

plantations large farms that grow only one type of crop, such as coffee beans or oil palms.

poacher someone who hunts an animal when it is against the law to do so.

pollinate to transfer pollen from one flower plant to another so that it can make seeds and grow into a new plant.

predator an animal that hunts others for food.

reptile a cold-blooded animal that lays eggs and usually has scales or plates on its skin.

reserves protected areas where animals can roam free and where the environment is carefully maintained for their benefit.

species a type of animal or plant.

swamps areas of water that are usually filled with plants.

wildfires fires that occur naturally but that spread very quickly.

Index

Numbers in **bold** indicate pictures

Quiz answers

1. Tropical and temperate; 2. Canopy; 3. To use the land for homes, farming or grazing livestock; 4. Javan rhino; 5. For their body parts; 6. Gibbon; 7. Three-toed sloth; 8. Binturong; 9. Chameleon; 10. Turtles and fish; 11. It is poisonous; 12. Climate change and disease; 13. Costa Rica; 14. Queen Alexandra's birdwing; 5. They keep the soil healthy, pollinate plants and provide food for other animals; 16. Hunting and capture to be sold as pets; 17. Bumblebee bat; 18. Global warming; 19. Pollution and declining fish stocks; 20. Elephant.